Minibeast Pets

Slugs and Snails

by Theresa Greenaway
Photographs by Chris Fairclough

WAYLAND

Minibeast Pets

Caterpillars   Spiders

Slugs and Snails   Worms

Cover photograph: A banded snail.

All Wayland books encourage
children to read and help them improve their literacy.

 The contents page, page numbers, headings, diagrams
and index help locate specific pieces of information.

✓ The glossary reinforces alphabetic knowledge and
extends vocabulary.

✓ On page 30 you can find out about other books and
videos dealing with the same subject.

© Copyright 1999 (text) Wayland Publishers Limited
61 Western Road, Hove, East Sussex BN3 1JD

Planned and produced by Discovery Books Limited
Project Editors: Gianna Williams, Kathy DeVico
Project Manager: Joyce Spicer
Illustrated by Jim Chanell
Designed by Ian Winton

British Library Cataloguing in Publication Data
Greenaway, Theresa, 1947-
  Slugs and Snails. – (Minibeast Pets)
  1. Slugs (Molluscs) – Juvenile literature
  2. Slugs (Molluscs) as pets – Juvenile literature
  3. Snails – Juvenile literature
  4. Snails as pets – Juvenile literature
  I. Title
  594.3
HARDBACK   ISBN 0 7502 2508 4
PAPERBACK   ISBN 0 7502 2512 2
Printed and bound in the USA

Find Wayland on the Internet at http://www.wayland.co.uk

Contents

Keeping slugs and snails

Slow-moving, slimy slugs and snails are not everyone's idea of pets but they are fascinating creatures. You will need to ask your parents' permission before you bring these 'pets' into your home.

▶ Remember to wash your hands after handling your minibeast pets.

Animal or tropical fruit?
This large banana slug lives in the United States. It eats all kinds of living and rotting plants and can grow up to 25 cm in length.

Slugs and snails have soft, legless bodies.

Snails make hard shells that their bodies can fit inside. Slugs are really snails without shells. But a few kinds of slugs have the remains of tiny shells on their backs.

Slugs and snails move along on a flat, slimy 'foot'. Their head is at the front end of the foot. They have four bendy tentacles, or feelers, that can be drawn back inside the head.

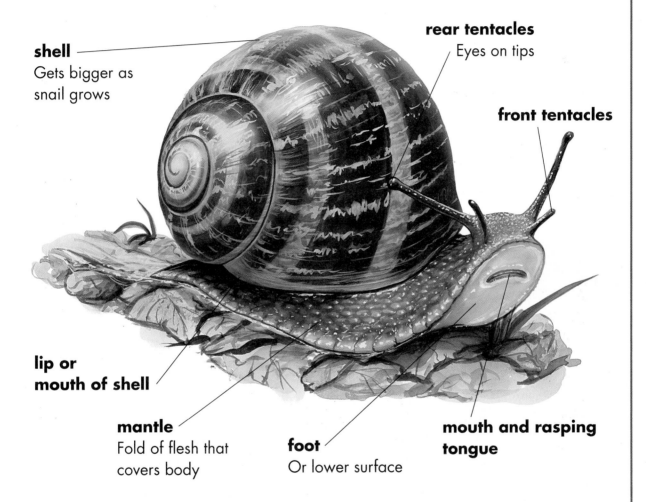

shell
Gets bigger as
snail grows

rear tentacles
Eyes on tips

front tentacles

**lip or
mouth of shell**

mantle
Fold of flesh that
covers body

foot
Or lower surface

**mouth and rasping
tongue**

Most slugs and snails have eyes at the tips of the two longest feelers. The shorter feelers are for smelling food. Underneath the head is the mouth.

Finding slugs and snails

There are many kinds of slugs and snails, and plenty of them, as any gardener will tell you!

Gardens have masses of tasty leaves for slugs and snails to eat, so they are easy to find.

Slime and froth

Although we may find their sticky slime disgusting, slime helps keep the bodies of slugs and snails from drying out. It also stops some animals and birds from eating them, because many predators do not like the slime sticking to their faces. Snails may produce a mass of froth when they are attacked.

Slugs and snails tend to live in damp places. They like ponds, riversides, and cool, moist spots in wooded areas.

They usually hide when it is hot and sunny and come out when it is cool and damp.

Some snails like water. Look carefully in a pond (make sure you have an adult with you). Can you see any pond snails climbing slowly up the water plants?

At the seaside, try looking in rock pools left by the tide. Sea snails often hide under seaweed, so carefully lift some up and look underneath.

▼ This is a great ramshorn snail. They live in ponds. They are normally dark brown, so this red one is quite unusual.

Slug and snail collecting

Slugs and snails move so slowly that collecting them is easy. You will need some jars or plastic containers with air holes in the lids.

You'll also need a pencil, some sticky labels, a small, soft paintbrush, and a flat lolly stick or plastic spoon.

Unless you live in a very damp area, you will find slugs and snails most easily if you go hunting in the evening after a shower of rain. Take a torch along, too.

Large snails can be picked up by their shells. Tiny snails have thin, fragile shells, so pick them up gently by rolling them onto a leaf with your paintbrush.

Slug slime is sticky, so use the lolly stick or spoon to lift them.

Put the slugs and snails into containers, together with a little bit of the plant they were eating. Label your containers saying where you found your new pets, and what they were eating.

When collecting pond snails use a small net. Put them straight into a jar of pond water with some pondweed.

Sea snails collected from rock pools must be kept in sea water.

Identifying your pets

To see which kinds of slugs and snails you have collected, you will need a magnifying glass, a ruler and a notebook. Books on slugs and snails, seashells, pond life, and even gardening books, may contain information on how to identify your new pets.

To identify a slug or snail, first take some notes. How big is it? Measure the snail's shell and the length of its outstretched body. What colour is it? Is there a pattern on its shell or body?

What shape is its shell? Some snails have flat, coiled shells. Others have rounded spirals or tall, pointed spirals.

Make a collection of empty shells. You will find lots of shells washed up on a beach. Not all of them will be snails' shells, though.

Carefully wash and dry your empty shells or they will start to smell.

Keep a record of each shell and make notes about it in your notebook.

Beautiful sea snails

Many tropical sea snail shells have bright colours and interesting shapes. Some periwinkles, like the snail below, have brown, green, or even bright yellow shells.

Ask an adult to help you check details of colour and size.

Slug and snail homes

You will need to make homes for your new pets.
Glass jars with lids are fine for the smaller animals.
Put a little bit of soil and a small tuft of grass at the
bottom of each jar. Don't forget to make air holes
in the lids, so that the slugs or snails can breathe.

To watch bigger slugs and snails properly you will
need a large, see-through container with a lid, such as
an aquarium. Put 5 to 8 cm of soil in the bottom.

Plant small tufts of grass and little plants in the soil. Sprinkle the soil with water to make it moist. Then add a layer of leaf litter. Make shelters out of pieces of tile, or flowerpots.

Put the lid on the container and make sure it is not left in bright sunshine.

Pond snails will be happy in a small aquarium with plenty of pondweed. Put a layer of sand or gravel at the bottom of the aquarium, and slowly fill it with pond water. Keep it somewhere light, or the pondweed will die, but do not let it get too warm.

Sea water soon becomes stale when kept in a container, so do not keep sea snails longer than a few hours or they will die.

Caring for slugs and snails

Common slugs and snails are easy to look after. Nearly all kinds eat living or dead plants.

Put little piles of different things – lettuce, potato peel, cake crumbs, an apple core – into their containers. See which type of food each animal likes best.

Remove uneaten food after a day or so, otherwise it will go mouldy.

Slugs and snails feel safer in dim light. They will not come out to feed in the bright sunlight.

▶ A cross-section of a snail's mouth, showing the teeth on the radula.

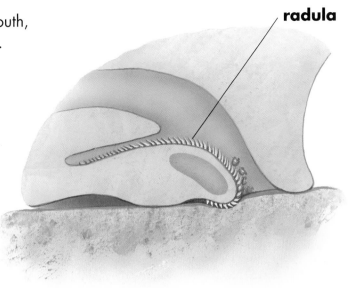

radula

Slugs and snails feed using long, rough tongues called radulas. The radula is covered with rows of tiny, hard teeth, which scrape the surface off the food.

Watch how slugs and snails use their tentacles to find food. Waving its tentacles gently, the slug or snail picks up the scent of the food and starts to glide slowly towards it. Sometimes it stops to test the air again, to make sure it is going the right way.

▶ Many toadstools are poisonous to people, but they do not harm slugs, such as this leopard slug.

Slug and snail behaviour

When a snail wants to move, its head and foot come out of the shell, but the rest of its body stays inside.

Try putting slugs and snails on glass. Look through the glass to see how they glide along.

Inside each foot are bands of muscles. These contract, one after the other, so that a wave runs along the foot. This moves the animal forward, little by little. Can you see the muscles moving?

Slugs and snails cannot see clearly with their tiny eyes, but they can tell the difference between bright and dim light. Watch what happens when you shine a bright light on a slug or snail.

After feeding, slugs and snails rest in a sheltered place out of sight of enemies.

To find out if snails return to the same shelters, mark their shells with little dots of nail polish or waterproof paint.

Silver trails

Glands just below the head of a slug or snail produce a lot of thick mucus. The animal moves along on this ribbon of slime, which protects its soft foot from damage and allows it to cross dry surfaces. As the slime dries, it leaves a telltale silver trail.

Pets or pests?

Most gardeners dislike slugs and snails. Not only do they gobble up seedlings and prize vegetables, but they also ignore the weeds! This is because many weeds are hairy, or have tough leaves, or a nasty taste.

Many garden plants have lost this natural protection. They are grown for their colourful flowers, or for their crisp, tasty leaves. Slugs and snails can feed on them easily.

▼ It is really disappointing to discover that a snail has eaten the flowers of your favourite plant.

But slugs and snails are not really villains.
Most will eat rotting plants as well as
living ones.

Shell crackers

Some birds have ways of separating snails from their shells, so that they can eat the soft bodies. The song thrush (below) hits a snail on a stone until the shell shatters. The snail hawk is a bird that lives in the United States. It has a hooked beak that it uses to remove large apple snails from their shells.

Slugs and snails play an important part in breaking down and recycling dead plants and leaves. In this way the nutrients they contain are released back into the soil. This activity keeps the soil healthy, which helps new plants to grow.

Reproduction

Most slugs and snails are neither male nor female –
they are both. But they still need to get together in
pairs to produce young. Before mating, they circle
around and around, making a large amount of slime.
As they glide around each other, they often touch.

▼ These two slugs, from a rain forest in Africa,
take a long time to get to know each other.
Before they mate, they glide around
each other in a slow and slimy
sort of dance.

◀ A Roman snail laying its eggs.

After mating, both partners crawl off to lay their eggs in damp, shady places. If the eggs dry out they will die.

Slugs often burrow underground to lay their eggs. Each batch contains between 25 and 50 round, white, pearly eggs.

The eggs take up to six weeks to hatch. The little hatchlings look just like tiny adults, with perfectly formed shells.

Slugs and snails have stretchy, slimy skin that grows with them. As a snail grows, it uses a part of its body, called the mantle, to add a new layer around the edge of its shell. The snail never grows too big to fit inside, because the shell is always growing with it.

▶ Snails grow tiny shells even before they hatch from their eggs. Each shell is very thin and fragile.

When winter comes

Slugs and snails find life difficult when the weather grows very cold. Their soft bodies are damaged by freezing temperatures. So where do they go in the winter? Try looking under flowerpots or rotting logs.

Hibernating snails often seal themselves into their shells with a layer of slime.

The slime forms a watertight cover over the mouth of the shell. This sticks the snail to a shed floor, or to the underside of a flowerpot, or anywhere else that is free of frost.

◄ This hibernating Roman snail has been turned upside down. You can see the hard plate of dry slime that seals its shell all winter.

Slugs burrow right down into the ground, where it is too deep for the frost to reach.

Slugs and snails may also burrow into the ground in hot, dry weather.

Eating habits

A few slugs and snails are carnivores. They are too slow to catch fast-moving prey, so they eat other slugs and snails, or earthworms.

Keeping a record

Your notebook is an important record of your slugs and snails. You will have learned a lot about them. Perhaps you know all about their likes and dislikes.

But there might still be things you'd like to know. For example, why does one snail's shell coil in the opposite direction to another's?

GARDEN SNAIL

Found: COMPOST HEAP
Date: 13 April
This snail was caught in the evening, after a rainy day. It was eating some lettuce. It is 2.5 centimetres long.

My snail likes to eat apples and potato skins.

GREAT BLACK SLUG
Found: Under a flowerpot
Date: 27 April

Why is one slug a different colour from all the others? Why do some pond snails always come to the surface to breathe, while others do not seem to breathe at all?

Taking a breath

Sea snails, and some kinds of pond snails, breathe underwater with gills that are hidden inside their bodies. Land snails and most pond snails breathe air through a hole near the edge of their shells. Slugs breathe through a hole in their side.

Libraries are good places to find out more information. As well as books, they have encyclopedias on CD-ROM, and the Internet. Museums with shell collections can be helpful, too. You could also to find out if there is a wildlife club for children in your area.

Letting them go

If you grow fond of your pets, you might want to keep them for a long time. This is easy to do with slugs and snails from your garden. They will be happy in the homes you have made for them. But all animals should one day be returned to the place they were found.

Pond snails will live in a freshwater aquarium, as long as you change the water whenever it becomes cloudy or starts to smell. Even so, it is is best not to keep them for more than two weeks. When it is time to let your snails go, take them back to their own pond.

If you collected sea snails, make sure you return them to the part of the beach where you found them.

In spite of their coats of slime, most tiny young slugs and snails are eaten by other hungry animals. Those that survive until they are fully grown may live for quite a long time. A few may live for ten years or more.

▼ A hungry beetle can put its head right inside the shell to eat the snail.

When releasing your slugs and snails, remember that they cannot move quickly to escape from predators, or the heat of the sun. The best time to let them go is on a mild, damp evening. Put them somewhere sheltered so that they can hide.

Slug and snail facts

Slugs are often crawling with lots of tiny creatures called mites. These scurrying animals do not seem to bother the slug at all. Scientists think that they just feed on the slug's slime.

◀ The largest snail is the giant African snail. It lives in the rain forests of South Africa. Its shell is 20 cm long.

The tiniest snails in the world are just 1.5 mm across.

Some sea slugs feed on corals that have stinging cells in their tentacles. When they are eaten by the sea slug, the stings pass into its skin. So any enemy that attacks the sea slug will get badly stung.

▶ The beautiful shell of this Haitian tree snail has stripes of many colours.

European great grey slugs behave in a very unusual way. When mating, each pair climbs up a bush and dangles in mid-air on a thick rope of slime.

▼ Some sea slugs are brightly coloured. This warns other hungry sea creatures that the slugs are poisonous.

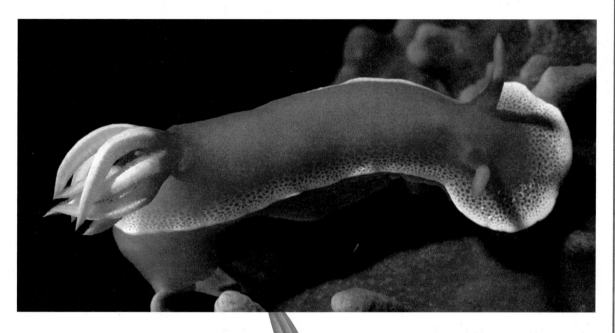

▶ Some snails have hairy shells. These tiny hairs are made from the thin, outermost layer of the shell.

Slugs and snails belong to a group of animals called molluscs. Scientists call them gastropods, which means 'stomach feet'.

Finding out more

BOOKS

Fun With Science: Minibeasts by Rosie Harlow and Gareth Morgan (Kingfisher, 1997)

The Really Horrible Horny Toad (and other cold, clammy creatures) by Theresa Greenaway (Dorling Kindersley, 1998)

Topic Box: Minibeasts by Sally Morgan (Wayland, 1995)

Wings, Stings and Wriggly Things: Minibeasts by M. Jenkins (Walker, 1996)

VIDEOS

Amazing Animals: Minibeasts (Dorling Kindersley, 1996)

Amazing Animals: Creepy Crawly Animals (Dorling Kindersley, 1999)

See How They Grow: Minibeasts (Dorling Kindersley, 1992)

FURTHER INFORMATION

CLEAPPS School Science Service will be able to help with any aspect of keeping minibeasts.   Tel: 01895 251496

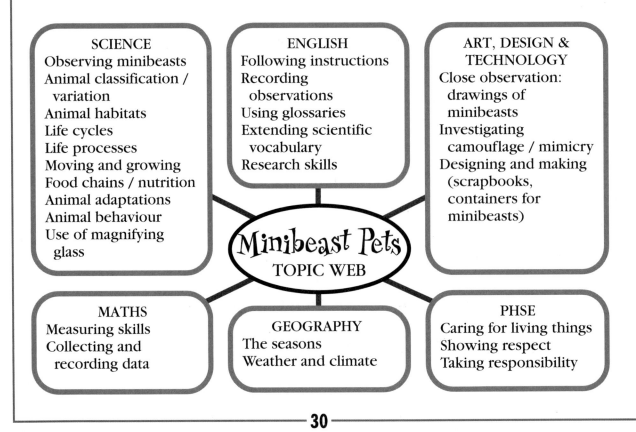

SCIENCE
Observing minibeasts
Animal classification / variation
Animal habitats
Life cycles
Life processes
Moving and growing
Food chains / nutrition
Animal adaptations
Animal behaviour
Use of magnifying glass

ENGLISH
Following instructions
Recording observations
Using glossaries
Extending scientific vocabulary
Research skills

ART, DESIGN & TECHNOLOGY
Close observation: drawings of minibeasts
Investigating camouflage / mimicry
Designing and making (scrapbooks, containers for minibeasts)

Minibeast Pets TOPIC WEB

MATHS
Measuring skills
Collecting and recording data

GEOGRAPHY
The seasons
Weather and climate

PHSE
Caring for living things
Showing respect
Taking responsibility

Glossary

carnivore An animal that eats other animals.

contract To shorten by tensing or clenching muscles.

gills Very thin-skinned organs that help water animals to breathe. They take in dissolved oxygen from water.

hibernating Spending the winter resting in a sheltered place.

leaf litter A layer of fallen leaves, mostly from trees.

mantle Part of the top of the body of a slug or snail.

mating The coming together of a male and female animal in order to produce young.

mucus Slimy liquid that animals produce from various parts of their bodies.

nutrients The chemicals that a plant needs to take from the soil in order to grow properly.

predator An animal that hunts and kills another animal for food.

prey An animal that is killed and eaten by another animal.

recycling Reusing a substance that has been used before for another purpose.

Index

The publishers would like to thank the following for their permission to reproduce photographs:
cover Robert Maier/Bruce Coleman, 4 Scott Camazine/Oxford Scientific Films, 6 Ken Preston-Mafham/Premaphotos Wildlife, 7 Felix Labhardt/Bruce Coleman, 11 Jeff Foott/Bruce Coleman, 15 Kathie Atkinson/Oxford Scientific Films, 17 M. Nimmo/Frank Lane Picture Agency, 18 K.G. Preston-Mafham/Premaphotos Wildlife, 19 Kim Taylor/Bruce Coleman, 20 Ken Preston-Mafham/Premaphotos Wildlife, 21 top Jane Burton/Bruce Coleman, 21 bottom Dieter Hagemann/Oxford Scientific Films, 22 Robert Maier/Oxford Scientific Films, 23 H. P. Frohlich/Oxford Scientific Films, 25 Ken Preston-Mafham/Premaphotos Wildlife, 27 Dr Rod Preston-Mafham/Premaphotos Wildlife, 28 James H. Carmichael/Oxford Scientific Films, 29 Howard Hall, Oxford Scientific Films.